Does Dracula have a wife?
No, but he has a ghoulfriend!

Did you hear about the spook who wanted to serve his country?
He joined the United States Ghost Guard!

How is an Egyptian sorceress like ham and cheese?
They're both sand witches!

D1040502

By Jim Davis
Published by Ballantine Books:

GARFIELD'S BIG FAT SCARY JOKE BOOK

Created by
Jim "Voodoo" Davis

Ghostwritten by
Jim "Witch" Kraft
and
Mark "The Dark" Acey

BALLANTINE BOOKS • NEW YORK

Copyright © 1994 by United Feature Syndicate, Inc.

All rights reserved under International and Pan-American Copyright Conventions. Published in the United States of America by Ballantine Books, a division of Random House, Inc., New York, and simultaneously in Canada by Random House of Canada Limited, Toronto.

Library of Congress Catalog Card Number: 94-94422

ISBN 0-345-38954-9

Manufactured in the United States of America

First Edition: October 1994

10 9 8 7 6 5 4 3

CONTENTS

FANGTASTIC FUN

What would you get if you crossed a vampire with Jon
     Arbuckle?
Count Dorkula!

Why do vampires drink blood?
Because coffee keeps them awake all day!

What do Dracula and a lollipop have in common?
They're both suckers!

What happened after Dracula appeared on *The Tonight
     Show*?
He received a lot of fang mail!

What did the polite vampire say to his victim?
"It's been nice gnawing you!"

Did you read the book about vampires?
No, I couldn't sink my teeth into it!

Why did the vampire go to the fast-food restaurant?
He wanted a quick bite!

Why did Garfield tell the vampire to gargle?
The vampire had bat breath!

Why wouldn't Dracula bite the old witch?
His teeth kept getting caught in her wrinkles!

What do you call an Egyptian queen who hangs upside
    down from the ceiling?
Cleobatra!

What did the Pilgrim vampire celebrate?
Fangsgiving!

Why did the teenage bat get into trouble?
He was hangin' with a bat crowd!

What is Dracula's least favorite day of the week?
Sun-day!

On what day does Dracula drink the most blood?
Thirstday!

What would you get if you crossed Quasimodo with a
flying mammal?
The Hunchbat of Notre Dame!

What would you get if you crossed Dracula with Odie?
A vampire who slobbers on your neck!

Why did the nurse send the little vampire home from
school?
He had a coffin fit!

Did you hear about the vampire's dog?
It was a bloodhound!

Does Dracula have a wife?
No, but he has a ghoulfriend!

What do bats wear when they get out of the shower?
Bat robes!

Why is a stuffed Dracula like three balls and two
    strikes?
They're both full counts!

What does Dracula want for Christmas?
Just his two front teeth!

What do vampires eat for breakfast?
Blood sausage!

What is crankier than a vampire with a toothache?
Garfield on a diet!

What do you say to a depressed vampire?
"Fang in there!"

What do you get when you cross a ball and a bat?
If you're lucky, a home run!

Why was the vampire put in jail?
He tried to rob a blood bank!

Why was the little vampire held back a grade in school?
He flunked his blood test!

What is a vampire's favorite Christmas song?
"I'm Dreaming of a Bite Christmas."

How is a vampire's breath like a congested man?
They both smell bad!

What is Dracula's favorite line for meeting girls?
"Hey, Gorgeous. What's your blood type?"

Was Dracula insane?
No, he was just a little batty!

Did you hear the one about the toothless vampire?
It was pointless!

How is Odie like a fangless vampire?
His breath is worse than his bite!

What is Dracula's favorite fruit?
Neck-tarines!

What is Dracula's favorite animal?
A giraffe!

How did the butcher attempt to kill the vampire?
He tried to drive a steak through his heart!

Why does Dracula wear a tuxedo?
Because he'd look silly in an evening gown!

How come vampires never seem to have any friends?
Because they're a pain in the neck!

What would you get if you crossed Dracula with wimpy
Jon?
A vampire who faints at the sight of blood!

How is a vampire like an artist?
They can both draw blood!

What were the vampire couple doing in the backseat of
the car?
Necking!

How is Dracula like false teeth?
They both come out at night!

What flavor of ice cream do vampires like?
Vein-illa!

What would you get if you crossed Dracula with a famous skyscraper?
The Vampire State Building!

What would you get if you crossed a vampire with Bob Hope?
A comedian who sings "Fangs for the memories . . ."

Human: "So, did you kiss that girl you went out with last night?"
Vampire: "No, all my efforts were in vein."

If Odie were a bat, what kind would he be?
A dingbat!

How many vampires does it take to change a light bulb?
Are you kidding?! Vampires *love* the dark!

What type of restaurants do vampires avoid?
Stakehouses!

What happened when the vampire met the beautiful woman?
It was love at first bite!

What did Porky Pig say after he was bitten by a vampire?
"B-B-Bat's all, folks!"

WITCHCRACKS

Why do witches fly on broomsticks?
It's cheaper than flying commercial.

Why did the warlock find the witch irresistible?
She had incredible hex appeal!

What happened when the little witch misbehaved?
She was sent to her broom!

Witch 1: "How do you manage to stay so ugly?"
Witch 2: "I guess I've just been blessed with bad genes."

What do hungry witches do when they want fast food?
They use the fly-through window!

Garfield: "I'm starving. Could you make me a sandwich?"
Witch: "Presto! You're a sandwich!"

Did you hear the one about the witch's broom?
It's sweeping the country!

Why was the witch drinking a lot of water?
She was going through a dry spell.

What would you get if you crossed a witch's brew ingredient with a legendary football coach?
Eye of Newt Rockne!

How did the witch get around after she lost her broom?
She witchhiked!

What would you get if you crossed a male witch with someone who makes keys?
A warlocksmith!

Why did the witch move from Salem?
She was transferred to a coven in Witchita!

What would you get if you crossed a witch with Garfield?
I don't know, but you'd definitely need a bigger broom!

How is an Egyptian sorceress like ham and cheese?
They're both sand witches!

What do you call a witch who can control electricity?
A switch!

How many witches does it take to change a light bulb?
Just one . . . but she changes it into a frog!

Why did the witch put her cat out?
It was on fire!

What would you get if you crossed a witch with a master
    chef?
A twelve-curse meal!

What do warlocks rub on their blisters?
Witch hazel!

What's the difference between an ugly witch and an old horse?
One's a hag, and the other's a nag!

How did the witch trick Odie into climbing into her caldron?
She told him it was a hot tub!

What would you get if you cloned a witch?
Double trouble!

What do witches put on their hair?
Scare spray!

Did you hear about the witch who didn't learn to fly until she was thirty?
You might say she was a late broomer.

Why do witches fly on broomsticks?
Because chopsticks are too small to sit on!

Knock, Knock!
Who's there?
Witch.
Witch who?
Witch you'd stop asking questions and let me in!

What is a little witch's favorite subject?
Spell-ing!

Where does a witch have her hair done?
At an ugly parlor!

What do little witches like to read?
Cursery rhymes!

What would you get if you crossed warlocks with a
    group of mutant superheroes?
Hex-Men!

Why do witches wear pointy hats?
Because they'd look silly wearing football helmets!

How did Garfield anger the witch?
He used her hat to play ring toss!

What do you call a witch who has no mind of her
own?
Witchy-washy.

How do witches tell time?
They wear witchwatches!

What brand of watches do witches wear?
Timehex!

What do you call a sorceress who wins the lottery?
A rich witch!

Where do witches go when they get sick?
To the witch doctor!

What do you call two witches who live together?
*Broom*mates!

How do you make a witch itch?
Take away a "w."

What would you get if you crossed the Abominable
    Snowman with a witch?
A cold spell!

Why should witches riding brooms keep their tempers
    under control?
If they don't, they'll fly off the handle!

What would you get if you crossed a sorceress with
    Superman?
A witch with hex-ray vision!

What has a broom and flies?
A janitor smeared with jelly!

Do witches like instant coffee?
No, they like it brewed!

MONSTER MADNESS

What TV show is about shipwrecked monsters?
Ghouligan's Island!

What did Garfield say to the Loch Ness monster?
"Go jump in the lake!"

What is the Swamp Thing's favorite dessert?
A hot sludge sundae!

Where do little monsters play at recess?
In the ghoulyard!

What would you get if you crossed a spooky Broadway
      musical with a TV talk show host?
The Phantom of the Oprah!

What's big, ugly, and drools on the mountains?
The Abominable Snowdog.

What do monsters eat for breakfast?
Lice Krispies!

What do monsters eat for dessert?
Leech cobbler!

Why did the female monster go on a diet?
She wanted to keep her ghoulish figure!

Why do monsters eat people?
Because they're too dumb to order pizza!

What would you get if you crossed Odie with a monster?
A drool ghoul!

Why was Frankenstein acting so strangely?
His head wasn't screwed on right.

What happened when Garfield mooned the Cyclops?
The Cyclops got an eyeful!

Do monsters like nursery rhymes?
No, they like gory stories!

Did you hear the one about the Invisible Man?
It's out of sight!

What do you call two monsters?
A gruesome twosome!

Who is Garfield's favorite movie star?
The Blob. Garfield likes anything that can eat a whole town!

What television show do sophisticated monsters watch?
Monsterpiece Theater!

What would you get if you crossed a dog with a nine-
foot monster?
A monster who drinks out of any toilet he pleases!

What did the Cyclops say to his girlfriend?
"I only have eye for you!"

What does the Abominable Snowman like to eat for lunch?
Cold cuts!

What game do monster kids play?
Hide-and-shriek!

Why did King Kong join the army?
He wanted to learn gorilla warfare!

What would you get if you crossed a monster with Garfield?
A creature who thinks the beast things in life are edible!

What position did the monster play on the hockey team?
Ghoulie!

What do you call an ogre with teeth like razor blades?
"Sir."

What did Garfield say when he met the two-headed giant?
"What's up? What's up?"

What's green and lives in a Scottish lake?
The Loch Ness Pickle!

Did you hear the one about the Medusa's hair?
It's hiss-terical!

Did you hear about the zombie who hadn't slept in a week?
He was undead tired!

Jon: "What would you get if you crossed Frankenstein with a hag?"
Garfield: "I don't know, but it still wouldn't be as ugly as a dog!"

What do Odie's brain and the Abominable Snowman
   have in common?
Neither one has ever been found!

What did the monster say to his girlfriend?
"You're the only ghoul for me!"

If Leonardo da Vinci had been a monster, would the
   Mona Lisa be considered a monsterpiece?

Monster pick-up line:
"What's a nice gargoyle like you doing in a place like
   this?"

What's green, flea-bitten, and slobbers on Tokyo?
Dogzilla!

What did Garfield say to the Invisible Man?
"Long time, no see!"

What do you get when Godzilla walks through a vegetable garden?
Squash!

What do sea serpents eat for lunch?
Submarine sandwiches!

What would you get if you crossed Garfield with Bigfoot?
A creature too fat to reach down and touch its toes!

What monster was a Civil War general and later a U.S. president?
Ghoulysses S. Grant!

What would you get if you crossed one of the Founding Fathers with a famous monster?
Benjamin Franklinstein!

What would you get if you crossed Garfield with Godzilla?
A creature that eats Tokyo *and* Kyoto!

Which Canadian city do monsters love?
Monstreal!

What would Bigfoot be if he ate Garfield's dinner?
He'd be history!

What do you call a monster who wears sunglasses?
A cool ghoul!

Did you hear the one about the Swamp Thing?
It's all wet!

What would you get if you crossed Garfield with the Blob?
Two blobs!

What do monsters like to drink!
Ghoul-Aid!

What was that gray thing between Godzilla's front
    teeth?
Tokyo.

What did the cashier say to the Abominable Snowman?
"Have an ice day!"

Child: "Mommy! Mommy! There's a monster under my bed!"
Mommy: "Tell him to get back in the closet where he belongs!"

Why did the monster's feet get wet?
He forgot to wear his ghoulashes!

How do monsters like their eggs?
Ogre easy!

Monster Kid: "Mom, I hate my teacher."
Monster Mom: "Then eat your principal!"

What would you get if you crossed a monster with snake-entwined hair with Jon?
Medoofa!

What kind of cheese do monsters eat?
Muenster!

What's big, green, and lives in the Himalayas?
The Abominable Snow Pickle!

What amusement-park ride do monsters love?
The scary-go-round!

What do sea serpents eat for dinner?
Fish 'n' ships!

Why is Frankenstein such a bad dancer?
He was made with two left feet!

CLOSET MONSTER

I'm the monster in your closet.
Beware! Beware!
You can't see me in the darkness.
I'm there. I'm there.
Your parents say I'm nothing.
No doubt. No doubt.
There's no monster in your closet.
I'm out! I'm out!

GARFIELD AND THE MONSTER

Garfield met a monster
Whose face was gray and grim,
Whose eyes were like two bloody eggs.
And hanging from his chin
A glob of putrid yellow drool
That made the fat cat gag.
"Put something on your ugly mug,"
He grumbled. "Like . . . a bag!"

Garfield met a monster
Who had a loathsome jowl
The shade of rotten pumpkins.
And from his mouth so foul
A breath that Garfield shrank in fear.
"I should never start my day," he groaned,
"By looking in the mirror!"

VAMPIRE'S LAMENT

I don't mind being a monster.
I'll tolerate a cape.
I'll endure unheated coffins.
I'll accept a crepey nape.
I can handle vampire hunters.
I can bear with dizzying flights.
But one thing drives me batty:
I am sick of working nights!

FUNNY BONERS

Why did the skeleton join the motorcycle gang?
Because he was bone to be wild!

How is Odie like a skeleton?
They're both boneheads!

How do little skeletons get to school?
They ride the skull bus!

What skeleton was emperor of France?
Napoleon Bone-aparte!

Which bone of a skeleton is the funniest?
The humerus!

Witch: "Would you like a piece of my newt's-eye pie?"
Skeleton: "Thanks, but I don't have the guts."

Why did the skeleton go to the library?
To bone up on his studies!

Why do skeletons hate winter?
The cold goes right through them!

What would you get if you crossed Garfield with a skeleton?
Lazy bones!

What do cowboy skeletons have on their feet?
Bone spurs!

What would you get if you crossed Novocain with a skeleton head?
A numskull!

What musical instrument do skeletons play?
The trom-bone!

Why are little skeletons always losing their lunch money?
Because they don't have pockets!

What did the skeleton say to his girlfriend?
"I love every bone in your body."

When is a skeleton a coward?
When he loses his backbone!

Why wouldn't the skeleton fight Garfield?
The skeleton didn't have the guts!

How can you tell that a skeleton has been to the beach?
By his skele-tan!

What would you get if you crossed a wisecracking rab-
bit with a skeleton?
Bugs Bony!

Why do skeletons drink milk?
Because it builds strong bones!

How do you unlock a cemetery gate?
You use a skeleton key!

What did Garfield say to the skeleton right before dinner?
"Bone appétit!"

What's the difference between a skeleton and a skinny person?
One's bones, and the other's skin 'n' bones!

Did you hear the one about the skeleton?
It's a rib tickler!

What did Garfield say to the skeleton?
"I have a bone to pick with you!"

What is a skeleton's favorite amusement park?
Boney Island!

What do you call a skeleton who teaches class?
A skullteacher!

Why did the skeleton drink a glass of water?
Because his throat was bone-dry!

Skeleton 1: "I hear you got a good report from your doctor."
Skeleton 2: "Yes, he said I was the picture of death."

How do you make a skeleton laugh?
Try tickling his funny bone!

When does a skeleton weigh as much as Garfield?
When the scale is broken.

What kind of dishes do skeletons use?
Bone china!

When is a skeleton not a skeleton?
When it turns into a haunted house!

What kind of hats do skeletons wear?
Skullcaps!

Why did the skeleton have plastic surgery?
She wanted higher cheekbones!

How did the skeleton know it was going to rain?
He could feel it in his bones!

What is a skeleton's favorite Halloween candy?
Jelly bones!

What kind of crew works on a ghost ship?
A skeleton crew!

How does a skeleton call up another skeleton?
He uses the tele-bone!

Did you hear about the skeleton who went on a diet?
He wanted to take off a few bones.

What do you say to a skeleton who's about to go on a
trip?
"Bone voyage!"

KILLER
KNOCK-KNOCKS

Knock, knock!
Who's there?
Robin.
Robin who?
Robin graves. Can you dig it?

Knock, knock!
Who's there?
Tish.
Tish who?
Tish the season to be spooky!

Knock, knock!
Who's there?
Rufus.
Rufus who?
Rufus full of bats!

Knock, knock!
Who's there?
Odie.
Odie who?
Odie brain of de psycho is de-mented!

Knock, knock!
Who's there?
Weird.
Weird who?
Weird you get such an ugly face?

Knock, knock!
Who's there?
Brent.
Brent who?
Brent over like the Hunchback of Notre Dame!

Knock, knock!
Who's there?
Gladys.
Gladys who?
Gladys Halloween! Aren't you?

Knock, knock!
Who's there?
Juan.
Juan who?
Juan to go trick-or-treating?

Knock, knock!
Who's there?
Les.
Les who?
Les pull some pranks!

Knock, knock!
Who's there?
Terence.
Terence who?
Terence a full moon tonight!

Knock, knock!
Who's there?
Hal.
Hal who?
Hal like a werewolf!

Knock, knock!
Who's there?
Heidi.
Heidi who?
Heidi your candy. Here comes Garfield!

Knock, knock!
Who's there?
Ghost.
Ghost who?
Ghost make me a boo-loney sandwich!

Knock, knock!
Who's there?
Randall.
Randall who?
Randall the way home to watch *The Addams Family*.

Knock, knock!
Who's there?
Lena.
Lena who?
Lena little closer and I'll tell you a ghost story!

Knock, knock!
Who's there?
Stan.
Stan who?
Stan still—there's a spider on your head!

Knock, knock!
Who's there?
Howard.
Howard who?
Howard I know . . . I'm just a mindless monster!

Knock, knock!
Who's there?
Yul.
Yul who?
Yul be sorry if you don't open the door!

Knock, knock!
Who's there?
Matt.
Matt who?
Matt scientist! Can I interest you in a brain transplant?

Knock, knock!
Who's there?
Olive.
Olive who?
Olive scary stories! Don't you?

Knock, knock!
Who's there?
King Kong!
King Kong who?
King Kong the witch is dead!

Knock, knock!
Who's there?
Goblin.
Goblin who?
Goblin food is what Garfield does best!

Knock, knock!
Who's there?
Amy.
Amy who?
Amy-tyville Horror!

Knock, knock!
Who's there?
Gus.
Gus who?
Gus what costume I'm wearing!

Knock, knock!
Who's there?
Gwen.
Gwen who?
Gwen the house. Here comes Dracula!

Knock, knock!
Who's there?
Ivan.
Ivan who?
Ivan to bite your neck!

Knock, knock!
Who's there?
Tomb.
Tomb who?
Tomb-morrow I'm moving to a bigger grave.

Knock, knock!
Who's there?
Linda.
Linda who?
Linda me your mask or I'll rippa off your face!

Knock, knock!
Who's there?
Igor.
Igor who?
Igor-geous babe is here to see you!

Knock, knock!
Who's there?
Oliver.
Oliver who?
Oliver the world people are scared of the dark!

Knock, knock!
Who's there?
Philip.
Philip who?
Philip my bag with treats!

Knock, knock!
Who's there?
Boo!
Boo who?
Stop crying and open the door!

Knock, knock!
Who's there?
Omar.
Omar who?
Omar goodness! Garfield ate all my Halloween candy!

Knock, knock!
Who's there?
Bea.
Bea who?
Bea-ware of things that go bump in the night!

Knock, knock!
Who's there?
Cher.
Cher who?
Cher your treats with me!

Knock, knock!
Who's there?
May,
May who?
May demons repossess your car!

Knock, knock!
Who's there?
Hugh.
Hugh who?
Hugh need a shave, Wolfman!

Knock, knock!
Who's there?
Crypt.
Crypt who?
Crypt up behind you! Ain't I sneaky?

Knock, knock!
Who's there?
Kong and Bess.
Kong and Bess who?
Kong-ratulations and bess witches!

Knock, knock!
Who's there?
Don.
Don who?
Don be afraid—be terrified!

Knock, knock!
Who's there?
Yeti.
Yeti who?
Yeti 'nother silly knock-knock joke!

Knock, knock!
Who's there?
Haunted.
Haunted who?
Haunted to stop by and give you a thrill!

Knock, knock!
Who's there?
Kerry.
Kerry who?
Kerry your candy?

Knock, knock!
Who's there?
Ron.
Ron who?
Ron for your life. Here come the zombies!

Knock, knock!
Who's there?
Demon.
Demon who?
Demon drove away in de car.

Knock, knock!
Who's there?
Fangs.
Fangs who?
You're welcome!

Knock, knock!
Who's there?
Anita.
Anita who?
Anita costume to go trick-or-treating!

Knock, knock!
Who's there?
Fright.
Fright who?
Fright my name down, so you'll know me next time!

Knock, knock!
Who's there?
Carmen.
Carmen who?
Carmen to get you!

Knock, knock!
Who's there?
Claws.
Claws who?
Claws the windows! There's a werewolf on the prowl!

Knock, knock!
Who's there?
Hairy.
Hairy who?
Hairy and open the door before the monster gets me!

Knock, knock!
Who's there?
Al.
Al who?
Al dressed up and no one to bite!

Knock, knock!
Who's there?
Boris.
Boris who?
Boris stiff with these stupid knock-knock jokes!

SCARED SILLY

Why did Lurch cross the road?
The chicken on the other side rang for him!

What would you get if you crossed a monster with
    Cindy Crawford?
A cover ghoul!

What show always scares Odie?
The Twilight Bone!

What sport do morticians bet on?
The hearse races!

What do you call an evil spirit that stubs its toe?
A screamin' demon!

What happened when Garfield crashed into the fruit
    stand?
He was berried alive!

What do Dr. Frankenstein and Arnold Schwarzenegger
    have in common?
They're both bodybuilders!

Did you hear the one about the grave?
You'll dig it!

What would you get if you crossed an athlete with a
    carved pumpkin?
A jock-o'-lantern!

What do demons eat for dessert?
Devil's-food cake!

Why couldn't Garfield read the letter from the Invisible
    Man?
It was written in invisible ink!

Do you like to watch scary movies?
I'm afraid not!

What's eight feet tall and oinks?
Frankenswine!

What would you get if you crossed a famous horror
    writer with a movie ape?
Stephen Kong!

When is a cannibal like an aardvark?
When he's an aunt-eater!

Did you hear the one about the maggots?
Gag me!

What does Elmer Fudd say on Halloween?
"Twick or tweet!"

What is Garfield's favorite type of Halloween candy?
Lotsa candy.

What famous American writer wrote scary stories and
poems?
Edgar Allan Poet!

What do gravediggers wear to work?
Any old thing they dig up!

What would you get if you crossed King Kong with a
prankster?
Some major monkeyshines!

Where do zombies live?
On undead end streets!

What would you get if you crossed Dracula with Binky
the Clown?
A vampire who laughs at the sight of blood!

Why did the executioner buy his ax on sale?
He was a smart chopper!

What do monsters in Budapest eat?
Hungarian ghoulash!

Why is Odie like a jack-o'-lantern?
They both have empty heads.

Know why graveyards have fences around them?
Because people are dying to get in!

What do you get when you cross a comedian with an undertaker?
Jokes you can really dig!

What professional baseball team is the scariest?
The Toronto Boo-jays.

What's orange and black and has a bolt in its neck?
Garfieldstein.

What was the monster's favorite bedtime story?
Ghouldilocks and the Three Bears!

When is it bad luck to have a black cat follow you?
When you're a mouse!

Why did the Abominable Snowman back out of his wedding?
He got cold feet!

Where do zombies swim?
In the Un-Dead Sea!

What happens to ghosts who tell bad jokes?
They get *boo*ed off the stage!

What would you get if you crossed Binky the Clown with a spiritualist?
A happy medium!

Why don't morticians tell jokes?
They're too busy discussing grave matters!

Jon: "A face like mine comes along once in a blue moon."
Garfield: "More like a *full* moon!"

What would you get if you crossed a vampire with a
    gymnast?
An acro-bat!

What bat tamed the Wild West?
Bat Masterson!

Did you hear the one about the ice pick killer?
It made my blood run cold!

Doesn't living in that haunted house bother you?
No, it comes with the terror-tory!

What kind of cheese does the Medusa like?
Gorgon-zola!

What would you get if you crossed the Abominable
    Snowman with a vampire?
Frostbite!

What has webbed feet and fangs?
Count Quackula!

Why was the little skeleton lonely?
He had no body to play with!

What do witches eat for breakfast every Friday the thirteenth?
Unlucky charms!

How do you make a milk shake?
Sneak up behind a glass of milk and scream "Boo."

Why did the Addams Family like having Thing around
the house?
Because he was so handy!

What would you get if you crossed a classic rock band
with zombies?
The Grateful Undead!

CREEPY COMICS

CREEEEEEEK

THE MUMMY AWAKENS FROM A SLEEP OF 3000 YEARS

AND SETS HIS SNOOZE ALARM FOR ANOTHER CENTURY

JIM DAVIS 7-20

BOY, AM I STARVED

I WONDER WHAT MUMMIES EAT?

WELCOME TO MONSTER THEATER!

TONIGHT'S FEATURE... "CURSE OF THE VAMPIRE GOLDFISH"

RALPH!..THERE'S A FISH ON YOUR NECK!

I LOVE THE CLASSICS

JIM DAVIS 12-12

AND NOW, THE LATE, LATE, LATE SHOW PRESENTS...

"NIGHT OF THE ZOMBIE PLUMBERS" IN 3-D!

I'VE BEEN UP TOO LONG

76

HYSTERICAL HOWLERS

What do little werewolves like to read at bedtime?
Furry tales!

Where do they make werewolf movies?
In Howlywood!

What would you get if you crossed St. Nick with a werewolf?
Santa Claws!

Why was the werewolf too embarrassed to go out of the
house?
He was having a bad fur day.

How does a werewolf get a thick, shiny coat?
He takes a bath in fur-tilizer!

Teacher: "How are werewolves made?"
Student: "With a wolf-fle iron!"

What would you get if you crossed the Wolfman with Jon?
A werewuss!

How many werewolves does it take to make a fur coat?
None. Werewolves can't sew!

Who helped the Wolfman go to the ball?
His hairy godmother!

What is the difference between a teenage girl and a
    werewolf?
One likes to shop the malls and the other likes to maul
    the shoppers!

What kind of beans do werewolves like?
Human beans!

Knock, knock!
Who's there?
Werewolf.
Werewolf who?
Werewolf I be without you?

What does a werewolf like to eat with his pizza?
A slice of delivery boy.

What would you get if you crossed a werewolf with General Patton?
A warwolf.

In what branch of the military do werewolves enlist?
The hair force!

What do Garfield and the Wolfman have in common?
They both wolf down their food!

Did you hear the one about the werewolf?
I was howling!

What has four fangs, ten claws, and twenty million split ends?
A werewolf who's run out of conditioner.

How is a werewolf like a computer?
They both have megabytes!

Why is a werewolf always late for a date?
Ever try styling the hair on your back?

What did the werewolf say to the barber?
"Just take a little off the elbows."

Did you hear about the party at the werewolf lodge?
It was a howling success!

How do you keep a werewolf from smelling?
Cut off his nose!

How many people can a werewolf eat on an empty stomach?
One. After that, his stomach's not empty anymore!

Which side of a werewolf has the most fur?
The outside!

What did Garfield say to the bald werewolf?
"Hair today, gone tomorrow."

How should you talk to a werewolf?
From as fur away as possible!

Who is a werewolf's favorite U.S. president?
Hairy Truman.

Did you hear about the lady werewolf who went broke?
She spent all her money on electrolysis.

What do werewolves call runners?
"Fast food!"

Did you hear about the man who turned into a ferocious pair of boxer shorts?
He was an underwearwolf!

What is a werewolf's favorite lunch?
A peanut butter and victim sandwich!

Why does a werewolf who has just shaved look like Pooky?
Because he has a bare face.

What would you get if you crossed a werewolf with a party animal?
A howl of a good time!

What do you have to know to teach a werewolf tricks?
More than the werewolf!

How do you get fur from a werewolf?
Take the next plane out of town!

What would happen if you crossed a werewolf with a bat?
You'd really see the fur fly!

If a werewolf lost his tail, where would he get a new one?
At a re-tail store!

What would you get if you crossed a cow with a werewolf?
I don't know, but I wouldn't want to milk it!

What's the best way to talk to the Wolfman?
Through the bars of a cage!

There once was a werewolf who didn't have a nose. Do you know how he smelled?
Awful!

Why did the werewolf bay at the moon?
Just for the howl of it.

Why did the werewolf have a tummy ache?
It must have been someone he ate.

Why did the little werewolf stay home from school?
It was a howliday!

What would you get if you crossed Garfield with a werewolf?
A furry monster who stalks your lunch!

Doctor: "Your arteries are nearly clogged. Do you eat a lot of fat?"
Werewolf: "Yeah, the skinny people run too fast."

What would you get if you crossed a werewolf with Neil Armstrong?
The furrest wolfman on the moon!

What would you get if you crossed a werewolf with a famous escape artist?
Hairy Houdini!

Where's the best place to keep a werewolf?
In a werehouse!

TOP TEN SIGNS THAT SOMEONE IS A WEREWOLF

10. You catch him sniffing your dog
9. If you even mention a full moon, he salivates to beat the band!
8. He can open a can of soup with his finger
7. He owns a silver-bulletproof vest
6. It takes him five-and-a-half hours to shave
5. You compliment him on his fur jacket, and he's not wearing one
4. He can't pass a graveyard without stopping to maul the old gravedigger
3. He excuses himself to go to the "Wolfmen's Room"
2. He has ring around the flea collar
1. You smell victim on his breath!

FRIGHT GAGS

Why do people carve pumpkins at Halloween?
Ever try to carve a grape?

What would you get if you crossed Odie with a ghost-
chasing cartoon dog?
Scooby Doofus!

What did Wayne and Garth say to the Invisible Man?
"See you later. NOT!"

How can you tell if a theater is haunted?
All the actors have stage fright!

How is a haunted house like Odie's breath?
One creaks and the other reeks!

What would you get if you crossed a monster with a Shakespearean play?
Romeo and Ghouliet!

What did Garfield say to the Abominable Snowman?
"Chill, dude!"

Did you hear the one about the horror flick?
It's a scream!

What did the cannibal say to the explorer?
"Pleased to eat you."

Hear about the new ice cream for monsters? It's called "Cookies and Scream."

Who do you call when your chicken is possessed by demons?
The Eggs-orcist!

How is Binky the Clown like Dr. Frankenstein?
They're both cutups!

What weighs a ton and eats tin cans?
Goatzilla!

What's the difference between Bigfoot and a doughnut?
You can't dunk Bigfoot in your coffee!

What monster discovered America?
Christopher Ghoulumbus!

What would you get if you crossed Odie's brain with
wimpy Jon?
Hollow-weenie!

What game do zombie children play?
Corpse and robbers!

Did you hear the one about Jack the Ripper?
It's a real killer!

When did the medium hold a seance?
Whenever the spirit moved her!

Why couldn't Garfield ever be a medium?
Because he'll always be an extra large!

Where do executioners get their guillotines?
At the chopping mall!

Did you watch *The Bride of Frankenstein* last night?
No, your sister had her curtains closed!

Did you go to the cemetery?
Yeah, the place was dead!

How did Jon scare Garfield?
He told Garfield that the pizza parlor burned down!

What do little monsters call their parents?
Mummy and Deady.

Teacher: "If I had eight pieces of Halloween candy, and
     I gave seven to my friend, what would I have?
Student: "You'd have a very happy friend!"

What game did Dr. Jekyll like to play?
Hyde-and-seek!

Does Garfield like to watch monster movies on his TV set?
No, he likes to sit on his chair!

Where do homicidal maniacs go to college?
Psychotic State!

What has two legs, a basket, and flies?
Little Dead Riding Hood!

What do you call pasta covered with bugs?
Vermincelli!

Why did Dr. Jekyll's chicken cross the road?
To get to the other Hyde!

According to Garfield, what day is the unluckiest?
Monday the thirteenth!

How do banshees like their coffee?
With scream and sugar!

What is a vampire's favorite food?
Fangfurters!

Jon: "Where are you going with that picture of Odie?"
Garfield: "To scare the mice away."

Why did the audience boo the vampire comic?
Because he was telling bat jokes!

What would you get if you crossed Freddy Krueger with
       a cat?
A dog's worst nightmare!

Did you hear the one about the Abominable Snowman?
It left me cold!

Jon: "What do Nermal and Dracula have in common?"
Garfield: "They're both a pain in the neck!"

GARFIELD'S TOP TEN NIGHTMARES

10. Nermal gets cloned
 9. Vet prescribes "chain saw therapy"
 8. Falls into vat of Odie drool
 7. Fleas vote him "Most Bloodsuckable"
 6. Inhales next to Jon's dirty socks
 5. Forced to watch the "All Lassie" channel
 4. Trapped for a week inside health food store
 3. Cat fur the latest thing for women's coats
 2. Meets huge spider with an attitude
 1. Diet Monday!

GARFIELD'S TOP TEN LEAST FAVORITE
HALLOWEEN TREATS

10. Saltpeter taffy
 9. Roger Ebert's leftover jujubes
 8. Chapped licorice lips
 7. Sweet 'n' sour porksickles
 6. Half a bagel some fat guy bit into
 5. Caramel watermelon on a really big stick
 4. Petroleum jelly beans
 3. Cookie crumbs from Geraldo's mustache
 2. Swollen gum drops
 1. Sugarless *anything*

GHOSTLY GIGGLES

What has one ear, carries a paint brush, and can walk
   through walls?
Vincent van Ghost!

What famous horror film featured ghostly chickens?
Poultrygeist!

Which city has the most ghosts?
Boo York City!

Cub reporter: "Is it true that there are ghosts in the U.S.
   Congress?"
Ace reporter: "Sure. Haven't you ever heard of 'Spooker
   of the House'?"

What candy do ghosts like best?
Boo-ble gum!

When is Garfield like a ghost?
When he's a gob(b)lin'!

What advice did Teddy Roosevelt give to the ghost?
"Spook softly and carry a big stick."

Why did the ghost see a psychiatrist?
The ghost was haunted by his past!

What kind of salad dressing do ghosts like?
Boo cheese!

Lady Ghost 1: "I heard you broke up with the Invisible
    Man."
Lady Ghost 2: "Yeah, I had a problem with his looks."
Lady Ghost 1: "But he doesn't have any."
Lady Ghost 2: "That's the problem!"

What would you get if you crossed a phantom with a
    cow?
Ghost beef!

Where do hillbilly ghosts live?
In haunted outhouses!

What do ghosts tell around the campfire?
People stories!

What fairy tale do ghosts like best?
Sleeping Boo-ty!

Rufus: "What makes you think this school is haunted?"
Doofus: "I heard everyone talking about our school
    spirit!"

What do goblins like to snack on?
Ghostess Twinkies!

What would you get if you crossed a goblin with Garfield?
A ghost that eats you out of haunted house and home!

Why did the forest ranger arrest the ghost?
He was haunting without a license!

What do spooks like to ride at the amusement park?
The roller ghoster!

What did the mother ghost say to her kid when they got in the car?
"Boo-kle your sheet belt."

"My crazy uncle has been seeing ghosts."
"He should see a psychiatrist."
"Why? The ghosts are cheaper."

What haunts your house and honks?
Poultergeese!

What would you get if you crossed Garfield with a
    specter?
A fat ghost that loves to eat spookghetti!

Who writes the best ghost stories?
Ghostwriters, of course!

What did the mother ghost say to the baby ghost?
"Don't spook till you're spoken to."

What would you get if you crossed a ghost with a fa-
    mous two-sport athlete?
Boo Jackson!

Where do spooks go to mail a letter?
The ghost office.

What would you get if you crossed a reindeer with a
    ghost?
A cari-boo!

Where do Appalachian ghosts live?
In the Boo Ridge Mountains!

How do you make Pooky spooky?
Add an *s*.

What do you call a ghost who styles your hair?
A boo-tician!

Did you hear about the spook who wanted to serve his
     country?
He joined the United States Ghost Guard!

What is a little ghost's favorite Easter activity?
The Easter egg haunt!

What does a ghost put on his pancakes?
Boo-berry syrup!

What did Garfield say to the ghost?
"Why don't you get real?"

What would you get if you crossed a ghost with a pirate?
Boobeard!

Knock, knock!
Who's there?
Spook.
Spook who?
Spook a little louder. I can't hear you!

Why should ghosts never tell lies?
Because people can see right through them!

What did Garfield say when the ghost told him an obvious lie?
"How transparent!"

How did the ghost look in her designer sheet?
Boo-tiful!

Did you hear the one about the phantom fireworks?
It was spooktacular!

What would you get if you crossed an amicable spook
    with a Capricorn?
Casper the Friendly Goat!

What kind of pants do ghosts wear?
Boo jeans!

What kind of ghost investigates crimes?
An in-specter!

What do you call a ghost on crutches?
A hobblin' goblin!

What's gross, slimy, and loves to assign homework?
The Teacher from the Black Lagoon!

Where do you find voodoo?
In the dictionary!

What would you get if you crossed Nermal with a psychotic maniac?
Abnermal!

What would you get if you crossed Garfield with a
haunted house?
Things that go burp in the night!

What branch of the military do zombies join?
The marine corpse!

How do you say "gremlin" in Swahili?
"Gremlin in Swahili."

Why did the executioner cross the road?
To cut off the head of the chicken on the other side.

What would you get if you crossed Halloween with Christmas?
A ghoul Yule!

What do Garfield and demons have in common?
One hates to exercise, and the other hates to be exorcised!

Which of the Great Lakes is the spookiest?
Lake Eerie.

What do evil chickens lay?
Deviled eggs!

Why did the sheep want to be tortured?
He was a mutton for punishment!

Teacher: "Use the word *phantasmagoria* in a sentence."
Student: "Okay. What does *phantasmagoria* mean?"

Where do gravediggers hold their annual convention?
Tombstone, Arizona!

What did Dr. Jekyll's mom do when he was a bad
    boy?
She tanned his Hyde!

What were the little monsters doing on Christmas
    Eve?
Troll-ing carols!

What monster was president of France?
Charles de Ghoul!

What does a hangman do every morning?
He reads the noosepaper!

Jon: "A face like mine belongs in the movies."
Garfield: "Yeah, *horror* movies!"

What do you call someone who puts poison in people's
corn flakes?
A cereal killer!

Did you hear the one about the giant?
It was over my head!

What would you get if you crossed the Loch Ness monster with an average student?
A "C serpent"!

How far can Garfield walk into a cemetery?
Halfway. After that, he's walking out!

What do you call a cannibal who eats his parents?
An orphan!

While serving coffee, what did the waiter say to Quasimodo?
"One hump or two?"

What would you get if you crossed Garfield with a female monster?
Gar-goyle!

What kind of hat does the Abominable Snowman wear?
An ice cap!

What time is it when Freddy Krueger comes to dinner?
Time to leave!

What do you call it when space aliens meet Jon?
A close encounter of the nerd kind!

What's the difference between a black cat and a frog?
A black cat has nine lives, but a frog croaks every
    night!

What is a vampire's favorite dance?
The fangdango!

What would you get if you crossed a ghost with Garfield's
    teddy bear?
Spooky Pooky!

What is Dracula's favorite sport?
Bat-minton!

What haunts the Paris Opera House and eats carrots?
The Phantom of the Hopera!

What happened when the Abominable Snowman tried
 to kiss his date?
He got the cold shoulder!

What would you get if you crossed King Kong with
 Garfield?
A creature too lazy to climb to the top of the Empire
 State Building!

What do banshees eat for dessert?
Ice scream!

What kind of shoes do baby ghosts wear?
Booties!

What kind of bears do you find at funerals?
Pall*bear*ers!

When Jon saw *Friday the 13th*, why was everyone star-
 ing at him?
He was scared out of his pants!

Why did the skeleton go to the seafood market?
He was looking for some mussels!

Do vampires like to drive on back roads?
No, they prefer major arteries!

Nermal: "How'd you know the Invisible Man had eaten your lasagna?"
Garfield: "I could smell the garlic on his breath!"

Why did the ghost visit the same castle every year?
It was one of his favorite haunts!

How did Bigfoot feel when he fell off the mountain-top?
He was crestfallen!

Which watches do rich witches wear? (Say this three times fast.)
Rol-hex!

Uncle Fester: "Why'd you tell everyone that I'm a doofus?"

Gomez: "Sorry, but I didn't know it was supposed to be a secret."

What is Thing's favorite sport?
Handball!

What kind of music do mummies like?
Wrap music!

Where can mummies always be found?
In the maternity ward!

How is Garfield like the Mummy?
They're both wrapped up in themselves!

Explorer 1: "Did you hear about Jenkins? He dug up a
priceless Egyptian mummy, then stupidly traded it
for a three-legged camel!"
Explorer 2: "Well, a fool and his mummy are soon
parted."

Did you hear the one about the Mummy?
It's ancient!

What do mummies do at their class reunions?
They talk about old times!

What would you get if you crossed the Swamp Thing
    with a bandaged corpse?
A scummy mummy!

Explorer 1: "Why would the Mummy awake after four
    thousand years?"
Explorer 2: "Perhaps he had to use the bathroom."

Why was the Mummy kicked out of the choir?
He couldn't carry a tomb!

Why did the Mummy steal the rolls of toilet paper?
He needed a new wardrobe!

How do you insult a mummy?
Rag on his bandages!

Did you hear that Odie is starring in a new version of
    The Mummy?
It's called *The Dummy*.

What would you get if you crossed a flower with an em-
    balmed pharaoh?
A chyrsanthemummy!

Do mummies like organic foods?
No, they prefer foods with lots of preservatives!

Who did the Mummy call when he broke his ankle?
The pyramedics!

What did the Mummy say to the Egyptian river?
"Nile be seeing you!"

What is the best way to get rid of the Mummy?
Call a surgeon. They know how to remove tombers.

Why are mummies good at keeping secrets?
They know how to keep things under wraps!

Why did Garfield tell the Mummy to relax?
The Mummy was all wound up!

Why did all the mummies get together?
To have a wrap session!

What happened when the Mummy ate the crackers?
He became a crumby mummy!

What do you call a business message from the Mummy?
A mummo.

Why did the Mummy miss the Halloween party?
He was wrapped up in his work!

What would you get if you crossed a mummy with a gorilla?
Kong Tut!

What do mummies eat for breakfast?
Shrouded wheat!

Why is it hard to wake the Mummy?
Because he sleeps like the dead.

Why did the investigative reporter follow the Mummy?
The reporter suspected a cover-up!

What happened when the Mummy was bad?
He got sent to his tomb!

How did Garfield diss the Mummy?
By insulting the Mummy's mummy!

Why did the Mummy send his mother flowers?
It was Mummy's Day!

Reporter: "Did the Mummy say anything when you opened his tomb?"

Explorer: "Yes, he made a few cryptic remarks."

What's wrapped in bandages and growls?
A hungry mummy's tummy!

Why did the Mummy start to take off his bandages?
He thought it was time to unwind!

Explorer: "What if I sell you my mummy now, but then later I change my mind?"

Museum Director: "Don't worry, sir. We offer a mummy-back guarantee."

Did you hear about the brother of the Mummy's mommy?
He was a mummy's uncle!

Why did the Mummy take his car to a mechanic?
Because the engine was out of tomb!

What is the Mummy's favorite cartoon show?
Tomb and Jerry!

What happened when the Mummy married the girl of
his dreams?
They lived wrap-pily ever after!

Reporter: "Have you ever found a mummy bigger than
this one?"
Explorer: "No, this is my maximummy."

Why did everyone run from the Mummy?
Because it had been four thousand years since he took a
bath!

Why was the Mummy placed in a straitjacket?
He was becoming unraveled!

What did the director say when he finished filming *The
Mummy*?
"That's a wrap!"

Celebrate the festive season with
America's funniest cat in

GARFIELD'S BIG FAT HOLIDAY JOKE BOOK

Created by Jim Davis
Written by Mark Acey
and Jim Kraft

What is Garfield's favorite thing
to put into a pie?
His teeth.

Why did Garfield take a nap in
the fireplace?
He wanted to sleep like a log.

Available in your local bookstore in
December 1994.
Published by Ballantine Books.

STRIPS, SPECIALS, OR BESTSELLING BOOKS...
GARFIELD'S ON EVERYONE'S MENU!
Don't miss even one episode in the tubby tabby's hilarious series!